Copyright 2013 by: Bernard M. Coyle

All rights reserved. No part of this publication may be reproduced, stored in a retrieval system, or transmitted, in any form or by any means, electronic, mechanical, photocopying, recording, or otherwise, without the prior written permission of the author. This Publication was printed in the United States of America.

Any comments about this Second Edition are welcome. Please direct them to:
Email: preambledefense@yahoo.com
Available on Amazon.com Kindle e-books;
ISBN# 978-0-9909661-4-2
In Paperback on Createspace.com
ISBN# 978-0-9909661-3-5
Under the categories:
Law>Constitutional
Religion>General
Other books by this author:
        "The Cancer Formula"
Categories> Medicine; Body, Mind, Spirit
Available on Amazon.Com, Kindle e-books and
Available on Amazon.Com, Create Space, Paper Back book.

I0159014

Table of Contents

PREAMBLE: IN DEFENSE OF THE FETUS
BY: BERNARD MARTIN COYLE

SYNOPSIS:

The Preamble states that the U.S. Constitution was ordained and established for ourselves and our posterity. Posterity means all succeeding generations. The only way to reach the next generation is the chain of life through human reproduction. The fetus is the most important link to the next generation. The fetus is posterity. Mr. Coyle points out that those who do not want the fetus; will dissect it as not being human. Whereas the entire world recognizes; at the first instant that a woman is said to be pregnant, she is with life; and will go through the normal nine month gestation required of a human being. The honored woman instinctively swings into action mentally and physically to prepare for the coming blessed event. She knows that her body is the cradle of the family's most precious asset – a human being and the next generation. Mr. Coyle also describes the legal chain of two human entitles; combining to make three entities, which morph into one legal human

1

entity - the fetus. Mr. Coyle describes how the U.S. Supreme Court erred; when it did not recognize the rights and responsibilities of the male; the rights and responsibilities of the female; the rights and the life of the fetus. Mr. Coyle describes in detail all of these rights and responsibilities. WITHOUT THE FETUS, THERE IS NO POSTERITY.

PREFACE:

This second edition expands upon the first edition. Mr. Coyle has introduced Part II THE NORMAL AMERICAN FAMILY. In it, he describes what takes place in a normal American family where a fetus is wanted; and compares it to the discussions in Part I, where the fetus is not wanted.

INTRODUCTION:

The primary purpose for writing this publication is to show legal justification for saving the life of the fetus. This justification was provided for by our forefathers when they wrote the Preamble to the Constitution of the United States of America.

THE PREAMBLE:

The Preamble to the Constitution of the United States reads:

We the people of the United States, in order to form a more perfect Union, establish justice, insure domestic tranquility, provide for the common defense, promote the general welfare, and secure the blessings of liberty to <u>ourselves and our posterity</u> do ordain and establish this Constitution for the United States of America.

TO OURSELVES AND OUR POSTERITY:

The Preamble states that the Constitution was established for ourselves and our posterity. Posterity means all succeeding generations. In order to reach the next generation from ourselves, there must be a recognizable Chain of Life. The Chain of life is within the Human Reproduction process, achieved by the unrelated male and female who consent to and perform the sex act. The product of the act, the Fetus, is the most important link in that chain of life from "ourselves to the next generation". In effect, the Fetus is our posterity.

THE FETUS AND THE CHAIN OF LIFE:

The human reproduces within a continual process for each human life. The process is: Consent, Performance of the Sex Act, Conception, Gestation and Birth.

CONSENT:

The right of consent exists because humans have a free will. The right of consent is an inalienable right.

Since reproduction of human life is a continual process, consent to the sex act is the trigger or beginning of the human reproduction process.
The act itself, artificial insemination, or any movement or action that achieves the natural result of the sex act, is a confirmation of consent. The duration of the act is insignificant.

The time of consent is the time of choice. Either party may choose to perform the act or not perform the act. The choice is made before performance of the act.

Consent is given by the nature and performance of the sex act between an unrelated male and female, assuming there is no violation of consent of either of the partners to performance of the act.

Both partners have a right to enjoyment of the sex act. Each time a couple consents to and performs the sex act, they acknowledge the possibility of and the responsibility for the reproduction of a human being, who is the product of their beings.

VIOLATIONS OF CONSENT:

When consent of the individual is violated, <u>certain abortion rights exist.</u>

(1) One party proceeds forcefully with the act, violating the other party's right of consent. This is when a <u>rape</u> has been committed.

(2) One or both parties are forced into the act by a third party or parties. This is when <u>coercion</u> is present.

(3)An adult performs the act with a minor who has not reached the legal age to consent. This is <u>statutory rape</u>.

(4) When two related persons perform the act. Whether one or two adults or minors are involved. This is when <u>incest</u> occurs. Incest is wrong because the product of the sex act is known to be a detriment to the natural order of life. It is a violation of consent because related persons have no right to give consent to each other.

(5)The act is performed with a person that has reached the age of consent but does not have the <u>mental capacity</u> to give consent.

NON-VIOLATION OF CONSENT - WHEN A CHOICE HAS TO BE MADE BETWEEN SAVING THE LIFE OF THE MOTHER OR THE FETUS.

In addition to the above, when a choice has to be made between saving the life of the mother or the fetus, the right of the mother is superior; because she would not be around to care for the fetus, which is an implied intent and requirement of becoming pregnant. She is a known quantity and can continue to contribute to society with or without having more children. This is especially true in the cases of married or committed partners who have or may have other children. She still has an obligation and a need to care and provide for the other children and the partner.

Growing up as a Roman Catholic, it has always been proposed, but not Catholic Doctrine that the fetus be saved because the soul of the fetus has not been exposed to life. I believe making the proposed choice to save the fetus and not the mother;

(1) Nullifies the prerequisite Sacraments to Matrimony: Baptism, Penance, Holy

Eucharist, Confirmation and Matrimony itself.

(2) It invokes Extreme Unction, leaving Holy Orders the only sacrament remaining.

(3) I believe the choice to save the fetus in Original Sin denigrates the authority and blessings of the Sacraments and their standing in the church.

(4) I also believe the choice to save the fetus rather than the mother is inconsistent with the church's stand on aborting the fetus on the occasions of rape and incest.

NON-VIOLATION OF CONSENT - BY MINORS:

Minors who have obviously reached puberty, who consent to and perform the sex act and are physically able, must be held accountable and responsible for their actions and carry the fetus to full term without the right to abortion. The minors certainly can care for the child after birth or place the child out for adoption. Carrying to full term is a burden but society must educate youth about sex and bringing another life into the world.

THE SEX ACT:

When married, a couple has a right to reproduce, which is accomplished by performance of the sex act. First, this allows the couple to share in the joy of the act, thereby forming a bond between them. Secondly, if the female becomes pregnant, it requires the partners to be present to aid and support each other during this trying time of gestation and throughout life. By the very nature of passing this right, society says you are partners and are equal in the right and responsibility for any results of the sex act. If a couple is not married, and gives consent, and performs the sex act, they assume all of the rights and responsibilities reserved for the married couple, granted by society.

Once the act is performed, and one partner decides to break the relationship, he or she is still responsible for the outcome of the sex act, whether it be a human being or not.

One or both parties cannot just accept the joys, pleasures and gratification of performing the act and then reject the responsibilities attached to the performance of the act.

Nor can the consenting female just walk away and not notify the male of the existence of her pregnancy, no matter how she feels about the pregnancy or the partner. Just because the fetus is housed and nurturing in her body, does not preclude the male from his rights and responsibilities.

Once the act is performed, all rights and responsibilities flow with and follow the product of the act. Neither partner has the right to ask, request or pressure the other partner into aborting the fetus. The fetus has his or her own inalienable rights as a human being and is entitled to have them honored by both parents and society.

CONCEPTION:

Conception takes place at the union of the male sperm and the female egg. Prior to this instant the sperm and the egg would have remained a sperm and egg if the union did not take place. Before and after conception, the sperm and egg are part of the parents, and carry all of the rights of a human being.   Because of the nature of the act of human conception, the male contributes ownership of his sperm and the female contributes ownership of her egg, to the creation of the fetus, this is an irreversible act.   At this instant they create joint responsibility for the fetus. Legally, the fetus is an extension of his or her parents, the sum of their beings, no matter how microscopic, and as such is a human entity. In effect, the fetus is three entities evolving into one entity on a sacred and constitutional journey.   All of the rights and responsibilities of the parents continuously flow from the parents to the fetus.   At the instant of conception, the link in the chain of life is complete. The fetus is the most important part of that link and as such is a human entity with his or her own inalienable rights. <u>The fetus is posterity.</u>

Once the union takes place, the encoded material in the male sperm and the female egg, comes to life and moves into action according to a plan of development for the anticipated human birth. The original encoded material directs the entire development of the fetus from the union or conception through birth, and the rest of the human's life.

WHEN LIFE BEGINS:

We know that a human being is produced after conception and that a human cannot be reproduced without conception. Recognition of the entire process of human reproduction is the essence of recognition of the chain of life and posterity. Presently, we dissect this process and acknowledge parts as they please us, in order to avoid responsibility for, or a reason to destroy the fetus. To say that a fetus is not human in the first trimester after conception or the second trimester is to say that the fetus appeared from nowhere. But, we know that the third trimester could not take place without the second trimester and the second trimester cannot take place without the first trimester and the first trimester cannot take place without conception. Reproduction of human life is <u>man's greatest act.</u> To ignore any part of the stage of development of the human reproductive process is to ignore the entire process of development. To ignore the process of development is to ignore the chain of life and posterity. To ignore posterity is to ignore the preamble and the constitution itself.

We know from experience that if the female does not or cannot take care of herself during even the earliest stages of pregnancy, the fetus can be harmed for life. If we recognize this, how can we say that life does not exist until some arbitrary point after conception?

GESTATION:

Generally, the nine month period, from conception to the birth of a baby. This is when the fetus proceeds to develop in the uterus of the mother, according to the plan of development in the male sperm and the female egg. This is the most vulnerable time in the life of the fetus and the Chain of Life   between ourselves and the next generation.

RIGHTS OF THE FETUS:

(1)The first inalienable right of the fetus, during gestation, from conception to birth, is the <u>right of safe passage, with a full escort – both parents being fully and completely responsible,</u> committed, caring for and loving the fetus. Society must recognize this individual right and at a minimum, do all in its power to protect the fetus in recognition and respect of posterity. To do otherwise, to harm or destroy the fetus, would be to act against posterity and the preamble of the constitution of the United States of America.

(2)The fetus has a right to be recognized as <u>a human being</u>. All of the rights of the parents continuously flow to and with the fetus. To ignore the existence and rights of the fetus is to ignore and show contempt for the entire process required completing the chain of life and the posterity of this nation.

(3)<u>The right not to be recognized as personal property of the female.</u> The Supreme Court of the United States in its ruling in the case of Roe versus Wade implies that the fetus is property to be disposed of at the discretion of the female. The question of the right of Female Privacy was considered. The female does have a right to her privacy as do all persons. But once a female consents to and performs the sex act, whether she enjoys all the pleasures of the act or not, she cannot claim to have greater rights than the male or the fetus. She has a right to care for her body but she also has a responsibility to care for the fetus. Her rights are no greater than the fetus except if her life is threatened.

RIGHTS OF THE MALE:

(1)The right to consent to or reject the performance of the sex act. <u>This is his right of choice</u>.

(2)Right to ownership of the male sperm.

(3)The right of notification when   the female is pregnant.

(4)The right to stop an abortion, because the fetus is also a part of him.

The Supreme Court ignores the rights of the male and the fetus. Even if the fetus were property, the court ignores how the sole ownership was passed or bestowed upon the female and what value did she give, to obtain sole ownership, to the rights of and the responsibilities of the male and to the rights and life of the fetus. Granted, presumably, she gave joy, pleasure and gratification to the male, but she also received it. If she did not receive it, by the act of consent, and performance of the sex act, both parties imply receipt, whether received or not.

RIGHTS OF THE FEMALE:

(1)The female has the right to consent to or reject performance of the sex act. <u>This is her right of choice</u>.

(2)Right to ownership of the female egg.

(3)The right to protect the fetus from abortion.

(4) The right of aid and full support from the male, including mental, physical and financial. The male must be held completely responsible for his part in the creation of the fetus and for the fetus during gestation and after birth, until the child becomes an adult.   The male cannot just walk away.

The female holds a special place and high esteem in society; because of her role in human reproduction, the raising of children, and as a partner to the male.   The female carries and nurtures the fetus during gestation, which is a burden. She also has the joy of feeling life within her. To the responsible females for whom this role in life was meant, the burden is accepted and recognized as an honor to carry the fetus to full term and posterity.

If a female were to try to cut her arm off, she would be stopped and shackled in order to prevent her from doing so. But if she decides to rid herself of another human being, the court will give her protection under the law. The court's priorities are out of order. It should be recognizing man's greatest act, the chain of life and the human reproductive process required to fulfill it. By doing so it will acknowledge the wording of the preamble, from "ourselves to posterity".

BIRTH:

This is when the fetus leaves the body of the mother and enters the external environment of other humans. The fetus is now a baby with all of the inalienable rights bestowed upon human beings at conception.

PART II

THE NORMAL AMERICAN FAMILY

In a normal American family a couple will go through a courtship, hopefully fall in love and get married. Ideally, they are the perfect match in the eyes of their families. At the wedding, the families of the bride and groom get to know each other a little better. It is a happy and joyous occasion. The couple may or may not be of the same religion; or not associated with any religion; they may be Spiritual people, who pray directly to God; Atheists who do not believe in any God. Whatever it may be, the two different families are committed to accepting the other party because they know it is best for both families and the bride and groom. The wedding then is a time of great celebration and the beginning of some lifetime friendships among the families and their friends.

After the honeymoon, the couple may live with one set of the parents or in an apartment or rented house. If fortunate enough they may have purchased a home. Whatever the case may be, each side of the families are interested in how life is going on with the new couple.

Then, one day the couple visits the doctor and are informed that the bride is pregnant. What a joyous and holy if not spiritual moment it is for the couple. Each gets on their phones to inform their parents, then their brothers and sisters and their closest friends. The parents in turn notify their brothers and sisters and close friends. What a Sacred and Joyous occasion it is for both families.

No matter what their religion, if any, everyone who has received notice of the pregnancy, accepts the fact that the bride is with life and there is no question or doubt about it. It may be only a month since the wedding took place but the bride is with life.

The wife immediately stops the intake of any alcohol or harmful foods to the fetus and prepares to keep her body healthy for the baby and herself. The bride and groom begin to prepare a bedroom for the new baby. This can involve painting and preparing structures for the day the baby comes home from the hospital. Both families want to get involved and help with the preparations.

On each side of the families, individuals wonder what or whom the child will look like. Will the baby look like the bride or the groom or one of the grandparents?

When the baby finally arrives, the excitement of the families hits its highest moment. This is the realization that the couple has received their greatest asset, that human being that just completed its mandatory gestation. The families realize that they have borne witness to the arrival of the next generation of Americans and indeed this is the flow of the lifeblood of democracy. This is the American Dream.

CONCLUSION:

In its decision in Roe versus Wade, the Supreme Court, in an effort to make the distinction among Federal Rights, State Rights and Personal Rights, chose to grant recognition of the Personal Rights of the female. The court assumed she owned the fetus. It ignored the rights of and responsibilities of the male and the rights and life of the fetus.

Further, it recognized that a woman has the <u>right to choose</u> abortion as a right entitled to her under the ninth and 14th amendments to the constitution, as a <u>right of personal privacy.</u> It ignores the fact that the woman <u>already had a right of choice and exercised it when she consented to and performed the sex act.</u>

Even if the fetus were property, the court ignores how the sole ownership was passed or bestowed upon the female and what value she gave, to obtain sole ownership.

As a nation we have suffered and continue to suffer the consequences of the Roe versus Wade decision. We see the lack of respect for marriage and the irresponsibility shown to the fetus and the mother. In our inner cities, as many as 70% of some of the males in ghettos do not acknowledge ownership or responsibility for the fetus; leaving the mother with the right of privacy to be the sole author of life and death of man's greatest act and to our posterity. If the mother grants life and cannot afford to care properly for the baby, the government will have to and does step in and accept responsibility. We know that this will only lead to future generations with even less respect for marriage, motherhood, life and our nation.

The greatest act that a human can make as a personal right is the creation of another human being. The court needs to recognize this in a positive way. The court needs to reverse the error it made in granting a right to destroy man's greatest personal act to create another human being. The court needs to recognize the rights of the male and the fetus. Legally, all of the rights and responsibilities of the parents continuously flow from the parents to the fetus. At the instant of conception, the link in the chain of life is complete. The fetus is the most important part of that link and as such is a human entity with his or her own inalienable rights. <u>The fetus is posterity.</u>

In Part I above we have seen how parents who do not want a baby, will go to great lengths to dissect the mandatory period of gestation. They will state that the fetus is not viable for some period of time which is only to ignore the rights of the fetus. Whereas in Part II, the instant that the mother is said to be pregnant, everyone accepts that the fetus is an unborn human being without question. This is the response all over the world and not just in America. All prepare to give the fetus safe passage with a full escort and recognize that a human requires a nine month gestation period unless it is born prematurely. Human births take longer because they are not flies or butterflies or insects.

Are we to assume that the fetus which is not wanted in Part I is a less than a human being than the fetus in Part II above; just because the parent or parents do not want the fetus; because it was only a product of their undisciplined discharge of their passions. Of course not. Both are human beings. Both are Americans. Both are the next generation of this great nation, protected by the Preamble and are the Lifeblood of Democracy. The Supreme Court of the United States needs to recognize this.

ABOUT THE AUTHOR:

Bernard Martin Coyle was born and raised in Philadelphia, Pennsylvania. Both parents were born in Ireland. He was educated in the Philadelphia parochial schools - St. Francis Xavier and St. Clement, under the direction of the Sisters of the Immaculate Heart of Mary. He graduated from West Philadelphia Catholic High School for Boys, under the direction of the Christian Brothers. At Villanova University, under the direction of the Augustinian Fathers, he received a Bachelor of Science Degree in Economics with a Pre-Law Major. He received his Master of Science Degree in Business, with accounting emphasis from the University of Northern Colorado. He enlisted and served in the United States Marine Corps during the Korean War. He and his wife Barbara Jo are both retired and live in Highlands Ranch, Colorado. Their children are: Christopher (and friend Carlene Simon), a daughter Kelly Marie Coyle Wyngarden, and Son Matthew (wife Britney Macklem Coyle). Grandchildren: Ryan and Chase Wyngarden; and Emerson and Bowen Coyle.

www.ingramcontent.com/pod-product-compliance
Lightning Source LLC
Chambersburg PA
CBHW060555030426
42337CB00019B/3552